Jane Williams is Assistant Dean and Tutor in Theology at St Mellitus College. She is the author of *Lectionary Reflections Years A, B and C* (SPCK, 2011), *Approaching Christmas* (Lion, 2005), *Approaching Easter* (Lion, 2006) and *Faces of Christ* (Lion, 2011). She is also a regular contributor to the Reflections for Daily Prayer series (CHP).

Little Books of Guidance
Finding answers to life's big questions!

WHY DID JESUS HAVE TO DIE?

A little book of guidance

JANE WILLIAMS

First published in Great Britain in 2016

Society for Promoting Christian Knowledge
36 Causton Street
London SW1P 4ST
www.spck.org.uk

British Library Cataloguing-in-Publication Data
A catalogue record for this book is available from the British Library

ISBN 978–0–281–07440–2
eBook ISBN 978–0–281–07444–0

Typeset by Graphicraft Limited, Hong Kong
First printed in Great Britain by Ashford Colour Press
Subsequently digitally printed in Great Britain

Produced on paper from sustainable forests

Contents

Dedicated to St Mellitus students,
past and present,
whose responses to my lectures on the
atonement have helped to shape this book

Introduction

There is no reason at all to doubt that Jesus of Nazareth was executed by crucifixion in the early decades of the Common Era. Crucifixion was routine under the Roman Empire, and Jesus' death is only remarkable in that it did not put an end to the disturbance he caused. Early Roman historians occasionally mention the Christian movement and its founder as a nuisance for the peace of the Empire.[1] So the simplest answer to the question of why Jesus had to die is that he annoyed the Romans. First-century Palestine was under Roman occupation, and the Romans dealt with any hint of religiously motivated unrest with efficient brutality.

Jesus' early followers cited Roman oppression as one of the reasons for Jesus' death. They also noted the involvement of the local religious leaders, who generally did not recognize Jesus as an authorized teacher of the faith and did not want to find themselves and their people in trouble with the Romans for something they did not even approve of. These Christian writers also accuse the ordinary people in Jerusalem at the time of Jesus of colluding in Jesus' death, roused to a mob mentality and baying for his crucifixion (cf. Matthew 27.21; Mark 15.14; Luke 23.20; John 18.40). Finally, they say that Jesus' own friends and followers ran away and left him to his fate. So another answer to the question of why Jesus had to die is that everyone around at the time, civic and religious leaders, indifferent bystanders and close friends, colluded in his death.

Yet the early Christian accounts do not think that human culpability is the whole story. They also assert that Jesus' death is divinely ordained, and they record Jesus as saying that his death is 'necessary' (cf. Matthew 16.21). It is because of this divine involvement, the New Testament says, that we continue to talk about this one particular death, not just as yet another example of human cruelty or of innocent suffering, but as something that, paradoxically, is part of the divine response to just that cruelty and suffering. Jesus' first followers testified that his death was not the end, that Jesus was raised from the dead and that they met him again. But the resurrected Jesus still bore the marks of the nails that had been driven into him to hold him to the cross. His resurrection did not wipe away his death, but it confirmed that Jesus, both in life and in death, is at the heart of God's action towards the created world and its inhabitants. It is because of the resurrection that we tell the story of Jesus of Nazareth. But the resurrection also confronts us, unavoidably, with the fact that Jesus died on the cross.

So we have a historical fact, with ordinary historical causes, and we have a theological fact with a divine cause, too. These two are not mutually exclusive, nor does the divine cause override the freely chosen human ones. God does not crucify Jesus Christ, human beings do. But Jesus' resurrection from the dead requires his followers to try to understand how God's Son came to die on the cross.

It makes the death of Jesus deeply mysterious and challenging. It does not fit into any readymade theological patterns or assumptions about how God acts. If Jesus is the Son of God, the question of why Jesus had to die becomes even more painfully unfathomable. But it is important to note that God is always unfathomable. To say that the action of God in Christ's death is mysterious is not to say something about the crucifixion that we do not say about the Incarnation or resurrection. The action of God is always mysterious, and the words we use about it are always less than precise, though that does not make them untrue.

The build-up to Jesus' death and then the description of it takes up disproportionate amounts of space in each of the four Gospels, and is spoken about by most of the other documents that make up the New Testament. Paul, writing to the Christians in Corinth, about ten to twenty years after Jesus' death, says that it will make no sense to most people, but that Christians know it is 'the power of God' (1 Corinthians 1.18). Clearly, the death of Jesus needed explaining and, in particular, people needed to understand why they were being urged to become followers of a crucified, defeated man. In response to that question, the first witnesses to Jesus tell about his life and teaching, his horrible death and his resurrection, and they tell it as a story that needs to be shared because it is the key to the saving activity of God. Jesus uniquely embodies the presence and action of God, so much so that it only makes sense if we say that Jesus *is* God. So Jesus had to die in order to bring the power of God to work in humanity. It is this latter assertion that we will be exploring in the course of what follows, but it is worth reiterating that the cross only has any meaning, over and above the meaning that any human death has, if it is true that he is both utterly human and yet at the same time utterly God,[2] and that he rose from the dead. Followers of Jesus, as they tried to make sense of what his life and death must mean in the light of his resurrection, began to realize that here was someone who was more than a prophet, who was, in fact, the presence of God, lived out in history, and even in death.

1

Why did Jesus have to die? The first witnesses

The writers of the New Testament, drawing on the memories and speculations of those who knew Jesus, do not have a clear, systematic answer to the question of why Jesus had to die. They record that the disciples were shocked and frightened by Jesus' death, and assumed that it meant that they had been mistaken in their identification of him as God's chosen one. They had no obvious religious framework in which Jesus' death made sense. As far as they could tell, that was the end of the story of Jesus.

It is only after the resurrection that Jesus' followers go back over his life and teaching and begin to try to make sense of what has happened. Jesus' resurrection is God's vindication of Jesus, God's claiming of all Jesus' life and death as, in fact, the work of God, and so now Christians have to make sense of why God allowed Jesus to die.

The disciples recall a few occasions on which Jesus seemed to suggest that he would have to die (cf. Matthew 16.21), though the disciples did not believe it at the time.

They notice the fact that Jesus did not avoid arrest, did not try to rouse his followers to fight for his freedom, but went willingly, if sorrowfully, to his trial and death. They also begin to notice the symbolism of the significant last meal that Jesus shared with them.

The Gospels agree that the Last Supper and Jesus' death are full of the symbolism of the great Jewish feast of the Passover. Passover remembers the mighty act of God to free his people from slavery in the time of Moses. This act of God brought them safely out of Egypt and constituted them as a nation again. So when Jesus shares the Passover meal with his friends, he is drawing on that set of profound allusions to the liberating work of God, which establishes a new, free people. But in place of the usual Passover lamb, Jesus puts himself. It is his blood, not a lamb's, that marks out the people who are to be saved.[3]

This supper has become one of the characteristic actions of Christians. It has its roots deep in Jesus' Jewish understanding, but it also has a new twist, given to it by Jesus' teaching and death. All four Gospels recount the supper (Matthew 26.26–28; Mark 14.22–24; Luke 22.17–20; John 13—17 is a long meditation on the Last Supper); Acts 2.46 shows the 'breaking of bread' as part of earliest practice, and Paul, whose letters are among the first written Christian documents, says that the tradition about the supper is part of the core narrative that every Christian teacher is required to pass on (1 Corinthians 11.23–26). Christians throughout the ages and throughout the world celebrate this supper, with its complex interweaving of history, death, liberation and the creation of a new people, as the defining ritual that gives us our meaning, and, unavoidably, at its heart this supper has the death of Jesus.

So the Passover imagery, reinterpreted through Jesus' own lens, provides some of the key themes for answering the question of why Jesus had to die.[4] It highlights God's action; it speaks of liberation from slavery; it uses the ancient rite of blood sacrifice; and it draws on the whole biblical account of God's relationship with the people of Israel. This is a hugely resonant and suggestive set of images, but not yet a clear 'theory', nor is it the only lens through which the New Testament makes sense of Jesus' death.

In 1 Corinthians 15.3 Paul reminds his readers that the tradition about Jesus says that he died 'for our sins'. Even more dramatically, in Galatians 3.13, he writes that Jesus' death made him 'a curse', or, in 2 Corinthians 5.21 that 'for our sake he made him to be sin who knew no sin'.[5] In this particularly challenging saying in 2 Corinthians, Paul is talking about an exchange made possible by Jesus: he is God's way of reconciling sinners to God; because Jesus becomes 'sin', we can become 'righteousness' and continue Christ's work of offering God's reconciliation. In 1 Peter 2.21–25 the same set of themes appear, suggesting that they were indeed widespread in the early Church. Peter says that the sinless Jesus takes our sins into death, so that we are now 'dead' to sin. Jesus waits on God's judgement, rather than human judgement, and that gives us, too, hope, as we suffer, because, like Jesus, our lives are judged by God, not just by other people. Jesus becomes an exemplar of hope for us.

This is such a complex web of ideas that it is extraordinary that Paul and Peter do not spell it out further.

They seem to take it for granted that their readers know this and understand it. Paul comes at this same idea in a number of different ways in several of his letters. For example, in Romans 5, Paul talks of the humanity of all who share in 'Adam', which is our humanity, sinful and ending, inevitably, in death; whereas Christ's humanity is righteous and obedient, and leads to life (an idea picked up again in 1 Corinthians 15.21–22), and we are offered a share in this new humanity 'in Christ'. In Romans 6, Paul links this web of theological argument to the Christian practice of baptism, which represents our admission into Christ's death, so that we are now living in a new humanity which is not enslaved to sin and death, but free to live towards the resurrection.

So this set of ideas revolves around Jesus as in some sense our representative and our substitute. In an obedience to the Father that contrasts with our disobedience, Jesus allows himself to be condemned to death as a sinner, condemned both by the legal authorities – the Romans – and by the religious authorities – the chief priests – and by the rest of humanity – his friends and the crowds – all of whom assume that God, too, has abandoned Jesus to his fate. He is willingly judged and willingly takes on the sentence of death. And that means that when he is raised from the dead, what he offers is a new kind of humanity – one that has been vindicated by God in the resurrection. We will explore representation and substitution in another chapter but, for the moment, in this New Testament context, what is being said is that there is a fallen humanity, represented by 'Adam'. We all share this humanity, marked by our wilful disobedience to God, and so our sad alienation from our true selves. Whether 'Adam' is a mythical or historical being, the description of the humanity that we all share still stands. Jesus, the Son of God, is born into this humanity and lives it, as we do, only in Jesus' case without disobedience to God. Since only God is 'naturally' alive, humanity that is not related to God dies, and Jesus accepts this death as part of his identification with our humanity. But since he remains intimately related to God, even in his suffering and death, his humanity lives beyond death, creating a new template of humanity. This is the new humanity offered to us through participation in Christ. It is a genuine humanity, lived in history, just as 'Adam's' is.

So in this pattern of thought, Jesus had to die in order to take 'Adam's' humanity into death and raise 'Christ's' humanity from the dead, as the start of a new creation. It assumes that death is the almost impersonal result of a humanity that has lost its anchorage in God, and is now unable to be freely itself. So human beings cannot seem to choose to be what they long to be: it is as though we are enslaved by forces that make us behave in ways that damage us and others. While the New Testament sometimes speaks of these forces as just the way the world is, it sometimes ascribes them to a deviant intelligence, actively working against God and human flourishing. Hebrews 2.14, for example, says that Jesus' death destroys the death-dealing one, the devil. In Colossians 2.14–15, it says that Jesus' death 'disarms the rulers and authorities', nailing their hold upon us to the cross. It is not clear that these 'rulers and authorities' are the devil, but they are certainly power-ful figures who believe they have enslaving rights over humanity. A similar idea is found in Ephesians 2.2, where the 'ruler of the power of the air' demands our obedience in opposition to God and to our own well-being.

So the humanity that dies with Jesus is an enslaved humanity, forced to behave in ways that are bad for it and which lead to death. Jesus' death is God's triumph over these forces, God's public assertion that humanity is now ransomed from these alien forces and returned to its true freedom in God's creation.

What is emerging, then, is a set of distinct but inter-connecting ideas about why Jesus had to die. They revolve around the creation of a new humanity which is no longer bound to an enslaving pattern of life that leads to death. They recall the character of the God who does rescue his people, as he did through Moses at the time of the exodus from Egypt. But they also confront human collusion with and active involvement in sinful and harmful patterns of life, and our willingness to be death-dealers ourselves. So there is a personal element to this – each individual is offered a chance to live the new humanity in Christ. There is also a cosmic element – the whole world is enslaved by powers that, because they are not God, cannot offer life and freedom. Personal freedom in Christ is bound up with corporate freedom for the whole created universe. They are two sides of the same coin.

But there is one further set of ideas that the New Testa-ment uses to describe why Jesus had to die, and those come from the ritualized sacrificial cult that is found in most human societies and that is detailed in Hebrew Scripture as a way of dealing with sin. The New Testament writers take this ritual for granted but, as with the Passover themes, it gets radically altered. The discussion is most clearly pursued in Hebrews, which focusses on the great ritual of the Day of Atonement. In Hebrew Scripture, this is described in, for example, Leviticus 16. Annually, the people face the terrible reality of their offence against God's law, God's justice, and God gives them a means of being truthful but not crushed by the truth. On this one day of the year, and this day only, the High Priest enters the Holy of Holies[6] and makes sacrifices for his own sin and the sin of the people. He also publicly lays his hands on the head of a goat which is then driven out into the wilderness, symbolizing the fact that God has removed the sins of the people, taking them far away. Leviticus 17 makes it clear that to kill an animal, to take its life, is always a meaningful act, and should always entail making an offering to God, too. God notes the taking of every life.

When Hebrews says 'under the law almost everything is purified with blood, and without the shedding of blood there is no forgiveness of sins' (Hebrews 9.22), it is simply stating a fact about current practice. But already within the Hebrew Scriptures this God-given ritual has a God-given critique: the prophets had reminded the people that the ritual is not a thing in itself, but a solemn symbol of the covenant relationship between God and the people (see Hosea 6.6, for example).

Repeated sacrifice was necessary because the people repeatedly wandered away from the relationships with God and with each other that were enshrined in the law. Hebrews says that Jesus' death is a sacrifice that does away with the need for any further sacrifice (Hebrews 9.26); Jesus offers his blood to God in place of all other sacrifices, 'to purify our conscience from dead works to worship the living God' (Hebrews 9.14).

We will return later to the complex of theological ideas here and, in particular, the question of who requires the sacrificial blood, but Hebrews seems to be suggesting that Jesus does completely what was done incompletely before through the ritual of blood sacrifice. So Jesus had to die in order to allow sinful, faithless people to remain in covenant relationship with God, while seeing and confessing the ways in which they have broken that covenant.

In 1 Peter 1.17–21 another layer is added to this image, by saying that Jesus is the perfect lamb, whose blood is offered as a ransom, a price, to rescue people from the old enslaving ways of behaving. This ransom is God's provision for our rescue from 'before the foundation of the world'. This is a different image from the one in Hebrews, in that it seems to draw more on Passover language than on Day of Atonement language, but the idea of sacrifice is here, too, with its assumption that some kind of payment must be made for sin.

This is by no means an exhaustive survey of how the New Testament writers approach the question of why Jesus had to die. But it does serve to bring out the main assumptions: that Jesus' death is necessary, not a horrible accident; that Jesus' death is God's action to liberate us and deal with enslaving sin; that Jesus goes to his death freely. Two things should be highlighted before we move on: the New Testament writers do not have one neat 'theory of the atonement'; but, at the same time, they wholly take it for granted that Jesus' death is the work of the love of God.

2

'Models' of the atonement

We have seen that the New Testament writers take it for granted that Jesus dies 'for our sins'. Their primary interest in this is to see how it has an impact on Christian practice and behaviour: how does it change the world we live in and the way we behave, if it is true that Jesus died 'for our sins'?

Building on the ways in which the New Testament describes the effects of Jesus' atoning work, a number of 'models' have developed. They are not alternatives but overlapping pictures, which help us to see how God works to reconcile us to himself and to free us from the things that prevent us from being our true selves. Some of these descriptions focus primarily on the 'subjective' effect of the work of God: its effect on us as individuals; some focus on the 'objective': the difference to the whole world; and some have both poles. Some speak of Christ as representing us in what he does: he does it on our behalf; others speak of Christ as our substitute: he does it instead of us. Again, in some descriptions, he is both a substitute and a representative. In all cases, Jesus can only do what he does because he is both fully human and fully God. In life and in death,

13

Jesus is fully identified with us but also brings into the situation something wholly new and creative, which is the work of God. Each model has its strengths and weaknesses: the main focus of the model is usually strong, but if it is treated as a total description it runs into trouble.

Jesus had to die to release us from captivity

This 'model' describes the world as enemy-occupied territory. Under this occupation, people are being forced to live in ways that are unnatural and destructive. We are not free to choose how we will live. God the Son comes to do battle on our behalf with the powers that are holding the world captive. He wins a victory over the occupying powers.

This model has the great strength of being anchored in Jesus' own life and actions before death. The Gospel writers show Jesus confronting 'the enemy' in his temptation in the wilderness (cf. Mark 1.13; Matthew 4.1–11; Luke 4.1–12) and asserting God's sovereignty over the world, in opposition to the devil's claims. They also describe Jesus' victory over the effects of the enemy's power, in the form of sickness and demon possession. In all his teaching, Jesus asserts the coming of God's rule, God's kingdom, where God's people will be able to be themselves again, owing allegiance only to God and not to the invading, destructive forces that enslave.

This confrontation with evil was not 'merely' spiritual. Jesus' teaching about the coming rule of God was a clear challenge to current structures. He spoke of a reversal of power of structures, so that 'the first will be last and the last will be first' (e.g. Matthew 19.30), he challenged the complacent wealthy (cf. Matthew 19.23), his 'manifesto' at the start of his mission (cf. Luke 4.18–19) was one of compassionate social revolution, and when he described his own leadership, he described it in terms of service (John 13.13), in contrast to the way in which leadership is normally exercised. So it is not surprising that Jesus' teaching was considered dangerous and subversive; it is more surprising that so many of his followers have not noticed its challenge.

So this 'model', building on the trajectory of Jesus' life and teaching, envisages a battlefield, in which Jesus is the commander of the army of liberation. His death is necessary because death is the prison stronghold of the enemy, and Jesus enters it to break it open and release those held captive. Death, the last enemy (1 Corinthians 15.26), is conquered. The decisive victory has been won and now there is just the continuing process of wiping out the last enclaves of the enemy.

This model has both objective and subjective aspects. Objectively, the world is in a different situation, in that the occupying forces are broken, if not yet wholly evicted. Subjectively, we are learning to live in our new freedom, and as we have been captive and oppressed for so long, this inevitably takes time. It also assumes that Jesus acts as a substitute for us: he does what we should have done in fighting the evil one.

The main weakness of the model is, perhaps, its militaristic language. But if we look carefully at the 'weapons' that God uses, rather than lazily buying into the battlefield imagery, then the strengths of this model probably outweigh its weaknesses.

Jesus had to die to ransom us from slavery

This 'model' is very similar to the battlefield model, but it pictures the scene of our captivity as a kind of slave market. All the other assumptions of the 'victory' model apply: we are held against our will by an evil master, and we are unable freely to be ourselves but are forced to serve our master. Jesus comes to pay the price to redeem us, to buy us our freedom.

The slavery motif makes strong imaginative sense. It harks back to the days when God's people were slaves in Egypt and God sent Moses to rescue them. And just as the freed children of Israel had to learn to live freely, and often complained about the vulnerability and responsibility of freedom and looked back to slavery almost with nostalgia, so we, too, are having to learn to live as free people, able to choose whom we serve and how. As with the victory model, this one also assumes an objective aspect to the work of God in Christ: the enslaved world is freed. This model also assumes that Christ is both our substitute and our representative. He does for us, as our substitute, what we cannot do for ourselves, in paying our ransom, but he also does it as our representative: it has to be a human life that is offered in payment for the enslaved human lives, so Jesus has to do it as one of us, not just as God.

This is the way in which Jesus himself describes why he has to die: he says 'the Son of Man came . . . to give his life a ransom for many' (cf. Mark 10.45), and C. S. Lewis famously picked up this description and gave it a moving fictional setting in *The Lion, the Witch and the Wardrobe,*

where the Christ-figure, Aslan, offers himself to be put
to death in place of the boy, Edmund. But while Lewis's
story shows what a powerful and helpful metaphor this
is, it also shows its weakness. In the story, the fictional
universe has an inbuilt rule that gives the evil white witch
rights over human traitors: her demand for a 'ransom',
a life for a life, must be met. As it happens, the witch
does not know that there is also an inbuilt proviso that
if an innocent person offers his or her life for a guilty
one, then the ransom demand is nullified. So the witch
is cheated of her prey.

Translating this from a vivid fictional account to a
biblical one is more problematic, particularly in terms
of some sort of bargain in which the devil has 'rights'
and in which God 'cheats'. So this 'model' has strengths,
provided it is not pushed too far. But if it is not pushed
to these logical consequences, then it is not clear why
Jesus had to die. If the evil slave master does not have
'rights' to the lives of his slaves, then why must Jesus pay
with his own life to buy us back?

Jesus had to die to transform our relationships and set us an example of obedient humanity

This 'model' is really a set of interconnecting models,
imagining slightly different settings, which could be
described either in classroom terms or in family terms.
The classroom setting goes something like this: Jesus
comes to show us what a properly human life looks
like, lived in unbroken and obedient relationship with

God. Now that we have seen this, we are invited to live it, in company with others. The family setting is similar: God is 'adopting' us into his family, and sends his own Son to begin to show us what it is to live in this family. The power of these images is in their trans-formational personal impact. Christians are encouraged to live new lives, inspired by the example of Jesus and in the knowledge that God loves us and wishes to make us his own.

The effect of this model is primarily subjective: we are changed. Jesus acts as our representative and example, showing us what a good human life looks like. There is a lot in the Gospel description of Jesus' life that supports this model: Jesus drew a close group of followers around him, taught them by example and sent them out to teach others. And the earliest Christians, too, seem to have grasped this as at the heart of God's work in Christ, creating a new community that lives in familial love with each other and with God. John 1 describes this as the result of the coming of Jesus: he gives 'the power to become children of God' (John 1.12).

While it may not be immediately obvious why Jesus had to die in this account, John 1 again helps to make the point. Strange as it may seem, many people do not want to be part of God's family, with its new way of life, and they reject the Son and put him to death rather than accepting his invitation. And for those who do understand and accept the Son, his death at human hands is a power-fully converting fact. We see just how much God loves us and longs to call us home when we see that the Son accepts rejection and a cruel death to make God's offer clear. As we look at the suffering of Christ, we are humbled and moved, so that this worst of human acts – the vicious cruelty of the crucifixion – calls out the best in humanity, too, our empathy and pity for the death of an innocent man, which makes us willing to change. Several of the great writers on the Christian life, for example Teresa of Avila and Julian of Norwich, testify to the fact that, in times of dryness and pain, the presence and companionship of the suffering Jesus was of vital importance to them: not Christ in glory at the right hand of the Father, but Jesus beside us in our broken humanity.

This set of interlocking ideas is probably the easiest for us to grasp: the death of Jesus is, in one sense, an accidental by-product of human indifference, but God is able to turn it to good effect. But the major weakness of the model is that, in objective terms, nothing much is different. The Hebrew Scriptures have always offered the love of God, and participation in God's family, and history is full of examples of good and faithful human lives. What is missing is that sense of constraint and enslavement, that something that prevents us from responding as we would like to. Without an 'objective' pole to the metaphor, faith is likely to remain a niche interest for those who are able to respond appropriately, rather than an act of God that somehow brings new possibilities to the whole created order. But a full doctrine of the work of the Holy Spirit can mitigate this weakness, because the Holy Spirit is the one who makes us more and more like Jesus Christ, praying in us and teaching us to be children of God, calling 'Abba', as Jesus does.

Jesus had to die to remove from us the sentence of death we have deserved

The 'models' we have looked at so far all depict God as acting to free us in Jesus Christ. We human beings are in some sense constrained to act and live against our own best interests. We may be powerless in this or we may be actively collusive with the enslaving forces, but either way God is on our side.

In this next model, we are made to face up to the fact that God is not indulgently loving, and that human sinfulness is not just personal but has damaged the whole fabric of creation. This model has as its setting the law courts. We, humanity, have been brought to trial for our crimes against the world and God. The evidence against us is overwhelming, and God, the judge, is bound by the statute book and by his own just and holy nature to condemn us to death. So Jesus offers his own death in our place. His offer is acceptable because, as the one through whom all things are created, Jesus can represent all of humanity: in his death, the sinful human race, 'Adam', dies. So Jesus dies both in our place and on our behalf, as a substitute and a representative.

This model is often described as though Father and Son have different attitudes to humanity. The Father is angry and needs to be appeased. But in fact, what is being said is that God, Father, Son and Holy Spirit, takes sinfulness with shocking seriousness but works to remove its full effects from us. God is still on our side.

If it seems harsh that there is any case against us and that God cannot simply wipe away sin, that may be because we have not truthfully faced the reality of the effect of injustice. If we think of children born to die because of poverty, or women raped as a routine act of war, it is hard to say that God should simply forgive the wealthy who just do not care about poverty, or the perpetrators of rape who have no thought for the humanity of the women they abuse. The God who simply forgives such things is a God who accepts that this is the way the world is and always will be. This is a God who is on the side of the powerful, and there is no hope of transformation in such a God.

But the prophets of the Hebrew Scriptures make it clear that God is a just God. He hears the cries of the oppressed and the ones whose voices we do not think are valuable. Jesus embodies this in his life and work, too. He challenges the rich and the comfortable, the ones who believe they have God on their side, and he seeks out the needy, heals the sick, commends the poor and confronts the indifferent. His trial and execution are a travesty of justice, so his resurrection is God's condemnation of the condemners. God publicly demonstrates that justice is not served in our world, and that when we face the judgement of our own lives and actions, our judge will be Jesus Christ, the one who suffered the injustice of human systems. The unjust world will be judged, and those who have suffered gross injustice will know that they are not forgotten and that their scars have been scored into the hands of the judge.

This 'model' answers the question of why Jesus had to die with the uncomfortable truth of justice and judgement. Jesus' death condemns us. But, paradoxically, that condemnation is our only hope of transformation, because in Jesus' life and death God is on our side. God confronts us with the reality of sin, and he upholds the cause of those who have been crushed by the sinfulness of the world, but then God offers to take the penalty upon himself in Christ. There has to be a penalty or there is no justice for the oppressed. But if we all had to bear the full penalty ourselves for what we have inflicted on others, then our case would be hopeless. Instead, what we are offered is a chance to live in the new community of Christ, where the truth of sin is fully acknowledged, as we break the body of our victim, over and over again, but where this truthfulness is lived in transforming relationships, as the Holy Spirit teaches us to be children of God and brothers and sisters with one another. The Christian world is one of truthfulness about the victim, whose face is always the one we see, whose cause is always the one we know God upholds, but that victim offers us the chance of forgiveness and transformation, because the victim's face is also Jesus'.

Jesus had to die as an atoning sacrifice for the sins of the world

It is hard enough for us to understand why God's justice might require that some penalty be paid for human sin, but it is even harder for us nowadays to understand the sacrificial imagery. This 'model' has as its backdrop the Jerusalem Temple, where sacrifices were made in order to regulate the relationship between God and human beings. It is tempting simply to dismiss this strand of the

New Testament understanding of Jesus' death as one that made sense in an ancient society that was used to blood sacrifice but that does not make sense to us and therefore needs to be laid aside. In particular, we find it distasteful to think that God demands blood in order to forgive.

But the Hebrew Scriptures do not say that. They say that God, in mercy, has always provided a means of reconciliation between human beings and God, and that that reconciliation is always costly, not because God demands that it should be so, but because the damage caused by sinful human beings is profound and far-reaching. The sacrificial system faces the terrible reality that sin is death-dealing. The Hebrew Scriptures nowhere say that God has to be appeased or propitiated: this is a means of reconciling us to God, not God to us. It is not God who cuts the throats of innocent animals, but us.

As with the legal 'model', the sacrificial 'model' makes us squarely face the fact that sin is costly. Day by day, human beings kill each other and devastate the world, God's world, with impunity, and there can be no concept of God worth having that does not demand some kind of accounting for this. This 'model' says that God takes all of this with such seriousness and sorrow that God the Son offers his own life as a symbol of all those lives lost, and as God's own way of making it possible for sinful human beings to be reconciled with God and each other without pretending that nothing has happened. In the blood of Jesus is also the blood of all the innocent who have suffered. God the Son brings them all, with his own blood, to the heart of the universe. This is what we have done, and continue to do, and God will not pretend otherwise, but nor will God sit helplessly by and do nothing. God makes a way home for us, facing our guilt but knowing that God has dealt with it.

'Models' of the atonement

These 'models', with their different 'settings', are not alternative accounts of why Jesus had to die. They are cumulative. God does not do one or other, but all and more. The action of God in Christ is still utterly mysterious, but with resonances that catch at our heartstrings and our intelligence and begin to give us insights into what it is that God does to reconcile us. The cross tells us that God will do whatever it takes to be the God of the oppressed and voiceless, the just and holy God, but also to be the God of mercy and compassion.

Each of these 'models' has at its heart a helpful idea, but if we take any one as the whole 'truth', then we come up against the paradoxical and uncontainable action of God that breaks all our images and models apart. God wins a victory through being defeated; God the almighty meekly offers himself as a ransom; God the creator of all things lives as a human being to show human beings the truth about themselves; God the judge offers himself for judgement; God to whom all sacrifices are offered lays himself upon the altar for us to dismember. God goes where our imagination cannot reach because our love is too timid and our words inadequate. Jesus has to die because our 'model' of God is tame and neat and can never reach the depths of our need.

3

The atoning God

The death of Jesus does not lend itself to any neat explana-
tions, in part because it revolutionizes our understanding
of God. Some of the questions that arise in relation to
the cross demonstrate how hard it is to allow the action
of God truly to dictate our understanding of God, rather
than to bring a prior understanding of God and try to
force it upon what God does.

The death of Jesus and the power of God

The Christian doctrine of God is that God is one, indi-
visible, but also three. So ways of talking about why Jesus
had to die that separate Father and Son are mistaken.
There has been a tendency to speak, indignantly, about
God the 'cosmic sadist', who chooses to inflict suffering
on Jesus. This is untruthful to the unity of action between
Father, Son and Holy Spirit, and it is also untruthful
about our own role in the death of Jesus. The Father
does not hammer the nails into the Son's hands and feet.
Nor is it God who continues to kill, maim, rape, starve

and brutalize people day by day. That is all the work of human beings. We are the cosmic sadists, the ones who inflict suffering, daily, on each other and on the universe.

God the Son comes to live in the world as we have made it, accepting the death that we choose to inflict. In doing so, the full power of God is on display. God, the all-loving, all-creating source of all life, is powerful enough to absorb the hate of human beings without retaliation, to accept the destructive force of human beings without disintegration, and to go into the darkness of death and emerge, still alive. And through all this, the love of Father, Son and Holy Spirit for each other and for us remains intact. In all things, God, Father, Son and Holy Spirit, is united in action, in purpose, in will and in love. Nothing that human beings can do can change God or prevent God from being God. Under all circumstances, God is loving, creative and living. That is why the death and resurrection of Jesus is the source of such hope: there is nothing that can stand against God, and God is able to take the tools of death and destruction and make them life-giving, make them a pathway back home to God.

Our own observation shows that God's 'power' is the only kind that transforms. All other uses of power, even in the service of good causes, perpetuate what they oppose. God's power, to be always God, unchanging, steadfast, loving and full of life, absorbs all violence and creates a new situation with new possibilities.

God's power is utterly respectful of human action and human purpose. God does not override our choices or wipe out our actions in order to restore harmony. But neither is God limited by what we can imagine. We think that the only way to overcome an enemy is by using similar weapons to those the enemy uses: force against force, anger against anger, fierce defence against attack. And so the sorry cycle of violence continues. Those who were oppressed now oppress others; those who were vulnerable now use force to ensure that they will never be vulnerable again, even if that force makes others as vulnerable as they once were.

God remains at all times God. God has possibilities that are beyond our comprehension and a power so alien that we barely recognize it as power. That power is symbolized by the cross. God is able not only to become human, which should be a contradiction in terms, but God, the source of life, is also able to die. But since the presence of God is always transformative, so God's presence in human life brings newness to humanity and God's presence in death changes its meaning and purpose. Humanity is no longer the opposite of divinity but its partner, and death is no longer the end but the beginning of new life. God takes what we are and what we do, and does not throw it away or overrule it but transforms it.

So the power of God is not divine force against human force, not a bigger power forcing a smaller one to concede; God does not compete with us for the reality of the world. He lives in and transforms the world as it is and as it has become.

But of course, there is more to it than that, because the world is not entirely of our making: God is still its creator. So Jesus had to die not just as the divine response to human action but also as the human response to divine action.

The death of Jesus and the responsibility of God

Even if we accept that God does not crucify Jesus or inflict the other sufferings that the world is full of, some of the blame must still be laid at his feet. God created a world in which these things are possible. In *The Brothers Karamazov*, Dostoevsky puts into the mouth of one of the brothers, Ivan, the objection that all have felt at one time or another. God could foresee, when he created the world, at least the possibility of innocent suffering. Should that not have deterred him from creating at all? Ivan invents the story of the Grand Inquisitor, who accuses God of giving human beings too much freedom, more than they could ever cope with. The Church has been trying ever since, the Inquisitor says, to put boundaries around that freedom and enable humanity to feel safe. The Inquisitor makes this passionate accusation to the silent figure of Jesus Christ, the Son of God, and Jesus does not answer him.

There is no 'answer' that God could give that would or should make human beings accept that suffering, particularly innocent suffering, is all right. But the Christian claim that the death of Jesus is part of the action of God to free and reconcile the world does put suffering at the forefront of all theological questions. God highlights it. God makes it his own most intimate concern. Jesus, God with us, is an innocent victim, like so many others before and since, and so when Jesus is raised from the dead, this is God's verdict – the suffering of the innocent is seen by God, and God makes it his own, and declares that it is neither forgotten nor is it the last word. There is more, beyond what seems like the bitter end, and that more is the life of God.

Jesus' death is God's free admission of responsibility for the plight of the world, as its creator. Although human beings freely do the evil that they do, as they freely crucify the Son of God, yet God has made a world with such terrible possibilities, and he himself enters into the reality that we have created. For Ivan Karamazov, and for many, many others, that is not enough and, strangely, God is on their side in that. God will not let us look away from the cross; for as long as the world lasts, this is where we find God, crucified but also risen, present in the world in all its reality.

On the cross Jesus cries out, 'My God, my God, why have you forsaken me?' In this, as in all else, Jesus repre-sents us. It is the age-old cry of human beings against what looks like the indifference of God to the sufferings of the world he has created. And God upholds this cry as justified. In Jesus, God acknowledges this as a just accusation. Jesus – with God's authority – speaks for humanity against God. In Jesus, God accepts that respon-sibility; God agrees that the world is broken and unjust and that human beings have a right to cry out against God. God makes this the central question of faith. Jesus, the human being who is also God with us, accuses God in God's name. In Jesus, God holds up all those who suffer and says, categorically, 'This is God's responsibility, God has not forgotten the cries of his people.'

The death of Jesus and the justice of God

In a world in which innocent people suffer and evil people go unpunished, the justice of God is in question. It looks as though God either does not care or is not sufficiently powerful to challenge this injustice. The death of Jesus is God's unexpected response to this.

Jesus is himself an innocent victim of injustice. The Gospels are perfectly clear that his trial is illegal and that he is condemned to death as a matter of expedience, rather than justice. So when Jesus is raised from the dead, the ones who condemned him are faced with the unpleasant fact that their illegal judgements have been overthrown by God. They thought they had had the last word and had got away with murder, but God's action proved otherwise.

Throughout the Bible, and perhaps particularly the prophets and the psalms, it is made clear that God hears the cries of the needy and the helpless, the poor and the powerless, all the people whose voices the world ignores or blocks out. In Jesus, God directly takes on their cause by becoming one of them, so Jesus is raised as God's judgement on injustice. In the powerful and terrifying parable of the sheep and the goats (Matthew 25.31–46), Jesus describes the judgement by the Son of Man, a name he often called himself. All who have mistreated or neglected the poor and needy will find that it is the Son of Man they have unknowingly mistreated. They thought these people were of no importance, and now they find that their whole fate depends upon them. The figure who sits at God's right hand to judge the world now wears the mistreated human face of Jesus and, in Jesus, all those who have suffered the injustice of the world. That is the image of judgement that the Gospels offer us: a face-to-face accounting with those we have injured, and who are upheld by the justice of God.

This 'law court' imagery has sometimes been described as though God the Father is the hanging judge, who agrees to accept the death of the Son instead of the death of all the guilty. But the picture is actually rather different. God, creator, redeemer and renewer, looks with abhorrence at the suffering we inflict on each other and hears the cries of the oppressed. Injustice is not to be accepted as the true state of the world, and those who practise injustice need to know that they will face the judgement of God, in whose presence will be all those who have suffered. Injustice is God's business, because it is God's good world that is being put into question.

But if the death and resurrection of Jesus is a terrible warning, it is also the source of hope, even for those who are condemned. God has overturned the unjust sentence of those who condemned Jesus and who condemn others daily. Jesus is risen from the dead, in order to restore and forgive. The disciples who betrayed and abandoned Jesus meet him again, and he offers them truth, reconciliation and a new mission. There is no vengeance in the risen Jesus, but equally there is no flinching from the truth. His disciples see the marks of the nails and receive forgiveness, and are then sent out to offer that to others.

So it is true to say that God accepts the death of Jesus as a means of suspending the sentence of death on humanity in general. It is true because what is offered in Jesus is an upholding of God's justice and yet also an offer of reconciliation to God and to those we have oppressed. In Jesus, God upholds the case of those who have suffered injustice, as Jesus did, and he requires us all to face what we have done, to see the marks of the nails. God does not 'just forgive', as though the suffering of the innocent were of no account; instead, God himself bears the suffering of the innocent in Jesus. Then, in return, he offers the whole guilty world a way of death and new life: repent, be baptized into the death of Jesus Christ and live the new, forgiven and forgiving life in the body of Christ.

The death of Jesus and the question of blood

As with the 'law court' imagery, so with the motif of sacrifice. The case has often been put as though God the Father requires the blood of the Son before he will forgive sinners. But just as it is not God who perpetrates injustices, but human beings, so it is not God who kills, it is human beings. In each case, God's action in Jesus refuses to avoid the reality of the world, but also refuses to leave it unchanged.

Life belongs to God. In the story of the murder of Abel by his brother Cain, the very earth cries out in horror when innocent blood is poured out (Genesis 4.10). Something has gone horribly wrong with God's good order when the innocent are killed. The sacrificial system, paradoxically, made the point clear: life is sacred; it is God's business when we kill, and we must account for it before God. In the Hebrew Scriptures, God is never placated or propitiated by the blood of a sacrificed animal;

instead, it is human beings who are reconciled by this action, which starkly represents their destructiveness and the fact that they cannot hide it from God. So God makes of our violence a means of truthful confrontation with its effects, but also a transformational act. God takes the death we make and turns it into a way back to reconciled life with God. So the sacrificial system becomes a prefiguring of what will happen in the death of Christ.

Death also makes an end. Blood sacrifice represents the putting to death of human sinfulness, and so the chance of a new start. In his own sacrifice, Jesus abolishes the ritual of sacrificing an animal as a temporary fix for sin, a fleeting new start. Instead, Jesus offers a permanent end and an unconditional new start, based not on our attempts to 'be good' but on God's willingness to deal with the past and create a new future. The New Testament speaks of the 'new humanity' that is 'in Christ'. Death has put an end to the old humanity that had to keep its own sinful accounts and attempt to remedy matters by the frequent putting to death of sinful ways. That humanity has 'died' with Christ, and the new humanity has risen in him. Death has been turned into life.

So it is true to say that the death of Jesus is a 'requirement' for the forgiveness of sins, because the death of Jesus is God's demonstration of just precisely how sinful the world is. Human beings are prepared to take lives, carelessly and callously, as though they were the ones with the power of life and death. Jesus' innocent death highlights human destructiveness. But it also highlights God's life-giving justice. There can be no transformation without justice. Forgiveness without confession is meaningless. God holds up to us a picture of ourselves, our violence, hatred, indifference and cowardice. It is writ large across the universe as Jesus dies at our hands. But God does not repeat the cycle of punishment that we have devised. God does not compete with us in condemnation and violence. Instead, God absorbs what has been done and makes it a way of reconciliation with each other and with God. When we truly see what we have done to each other, in the marks of the nails in Jesus' hands, then we know that we have no possible means of offering 'satisfaction' to the victims of injustice. We cannot give back the lives that we have taken. But God can. God raises Jesus to life, to confront and forgive his betrayers, and God will do the same for all who have suffered.

Jesus and the wrath of God

God is not bad-tempered, but there is a great deal in the world that God cannot countenance. If we think that God should 'just forgive' the monstrous, painful injustices of the world, that is probably because we have not ourselves suffered much from them. But when we hear of children abused, or gunmen opening fire on innocent crowds, or dictators who care only for their own wealth and power and not at all for the well-being of the people they rule, we may have some inkling of the 'wrath' of God. We human beings demand justice and an accounting; we do not accept that this is just the way of the world and it must be endured. The God of the Bible is a God of justice because without justice there is no hope.

Some ways of talking about the love of God have made
God sound like an indulgent grandparent, always willing
to make excuses for the bad behaviour of the spoiled
youngsters. But that is an untruthful love: it has to deny
reality. God's love, on the contrary, is searingly truthful,
and so transformative. God sees the reality of the world
and yet loves it, and the love of God is endlessly creative,
restorative and life-giving.

On the cross, Jesus endures the terrible pain and injustice of a world that has lost its anchorage in truth and
love. He suffers, as so many do, the 'wrath' of God, which
allows the world to bear the consequences of what it does
rather than constantly intervening. As a human being like
us, Jesus suffers, as we do, the consequences of the world
that we have brought into existence. He suffers God's
judgement on such a world. He does this willingly – there
is no sense in the Gospels that Jesus is coerced into this
path; much as he longs to avoid it, he goes freely to the
cross. Movingly, the Gospels also say that, like us, Jesus
feels abandoned by God, as though God does not care
about the injustice and the agony of the man hanging on
the cross. As Jesus cries out, 'My God, my God, why have
you forsaken me?' he is expressing human despair in the
face of the wrath of the God who leaves us to our fate.

But Jesus' death is not the end of the story. Jesus is
not just a human being, but also God, the Son. So God
has not abandoned him on the cross, because Father and
Son are one and cannot be divided. Unimaginably, God
the Son enters into 'wrath' – the consequences of sin.
God the Son takes on himself the full costliness of what
the world has become, in its injustice, suffering, alienation

from its true being in God, and death. But now the paradox becomes life-giving: God cannot be divided from God, so death cannot hold onto the Son; the sentence of death, the consequences of the 'wrath' and justice of God, is unravelled. Jesus is raised from the dead, as the one who has borne the full penalty of God's justice but survived, through the active life and love of God.

Here in the death of Jesus, God upholds the vital justice of the world: sin has consequences. But God is not bound to leave us to our hellish lives in order to demonstrate his justice. God has resources that we do not dream of, because God's truthful love is unbreakable. When God stands in wrath against the sinful world, he does so for our life and health. When God passes the sentence on sin, he does so to bring us out into new life.

Jesus' death for us, with us, on our behalf, in our place

In all that Jesus does, in life and death, Jesus is our representative. He is completely identified with us in our humanity, and he lives the human life that the Bible dreams of, where human beings can be image-bearers of God, as the Genesis creation story describes them. So, strangely enough, Jesus, the human being, is fully representing God as well. Here, at last, is a human being who actually is God's image-bearer, doing for us what we cannot do. This human life becomes not just an idea but a reality, lived in the history of Jesus. Those who respond to the call to be 'in Christ' are learning to live the life that Jesus has made possible.

But Jesus lives that truly human life under the conditions of the world that has lost its reality, lost its hold on God, and so Jesus has to suffer and die to share this life with us. But that then means that even suffering and death are full of the presence of God. God has made a way to be with us even in the grave, and since God is always creative and life-giving, that means that the grave is no longer our end. Those who are 'in Christ' are part of the eternal love of God, which does not let go, even through death.

In all that Jesus does, in life and death, Jesus is also our substitute. He does what we cannot do, on our behalf. That makes some sense in his life – he, unlike us, is able to live in unbroken relationship with the Father, and so to bring into existence the new humanity, in which we can now participate. But it is also true of Jesus' death. Since only God is 'alive', in the sense of having life as part of the divine nature, creatures that have become separated from God are bound to die. But in death Jesus takes the un-breakable love of God even into the realms of darkness, so that even death no longer has to separate us from God. Jesus takes on this death as our substitute, instead of us, so that now our own deaths do not have to separate us from each other or from God. Beyond physical death, we are still held in the community of the eternal love of God.

Jesus is our representative as he holds up for all to see a world that is not good and not right. Jesus screams out against God on our behalf. This is the unavoidable human question against faith, and it becomes the unavoidable divine question, too, since Jesus is fully human and also fully God. God agrees that this darkness and violence and injustice is properly met by a human demand for a divine response.

Conclusion:
Why did Jesus have to die?

The simple answer to the question of why Jesus had to die is the answer that could be given about the death of any innocent victim: Jesus had to die because human beings can be violent, cruel and unjust. He died because we are sinful, as so many others have died. Jesus died 'for our sins'.

But that phrase 'for our sins' also has another meaning in Christian thinking: Jesus died because God, the just and loving, takes action in Jesus in relation to our sin and its consequences. God's action does not overrule what we do – Jesus does die. But nor does it admit that our actions are the complete truth of the world. Jesus' death upholds another standard of justice, and it creates another set of possibilities that are not envisaged within the world of our creation. God enacts his own justice, while acknowledging our own challenge to his justice, while the world is the way it is. The victims are not forgotten or brushed away as of no account: Jesus stands as one of them, one of us, and as their champion, judging those who have wronged them and him. But the violent are also not left out of God's mercy: they are given the opportunity to see their victim and their God in the face of Jesus and to enter into a new world of relationships in Christ. They are offered the full acknowledgement of God, who made the world with its possibilities of damaging and being damaged. The endless creativity of God is at work even through sin and death. God who made the world from nothing is not constrained by what we have made of this world, and death no longer separates us from each other or from God, the source of life.

The death of Jesus is God's comprehensive and wholly unexpected response to the distortions and abuses of the world. They are real, but they do not determine what God can do. The cross is not an 'answer' to the problem of evil and suffering, but it acknowledges that problem as the heart of faith. We are right to see it as an affront against any notions of a just and loving God. While the world lasts, the figure of Jesus on the cross is the cross of God, who acknowledges the world's pain and anger as the responsibility of God. In Jesus' death, our accusations against God and God's accusations against us meet and are held together in the human being who is also the Son of God. But this is not stasis: this is not just a tableau of the conundrum at the heart of the universe, it is also the mighty and incomprehensible act of God, in the midst of the truthful reality of the world. Life pours out from this point of death, and a new community of hope arises.

The great seventeenth-century poet–priest John Donne wrote this in a sermon preached on Christmas day: 'He can bring thy summer out of winter, though thou have no spring.' We know this because he brought Jesus from death to life.

Notes

1 Cf. Suetonius, *Life of Claudius*, XXV.4; *Life of Nero*, XVI.2. Tacitus, *Annals*, XV.44.2–8, specially 'Christus . . . suffered the extreme penalty during the reign of Tiberius'.
2 There is not space here to set out the reasons for believing that Jesus Christ is the Son of God, the Second Person of the Trinity. But who he is cannot be separated from what he does: his life, death and resurrection are the reason why Christians say that God is properly named as Father, Son and Holy Spirit, one God in three persons.
3 Read the story in Exodus 12.
4 Paul Bradshaw does not believe that the death of Jesus is the key to the Christian practice of the Eucharist (cf. Paul Bradshaw and Maxwell E. Johnson, *The Eucharistic Liturgies: Their evolution and interpretation*, London: SPCK, 2012, ch. 1 'Origins'). He is unusual in this respect.
5 Jurgen Moltmann clearly sets out the ways in which Jesus' death identifies him with blasphemers, rebels and the godforsaken (cf. *The Crucified God*, London: SCM Press, 1974, pp. 130ff). Jesus becomes 'sin'. Moltmann sees this as God's presence with and identification with those who are considered outcasts, thereby casting doubt on human judgements.
6 The Temple in Jerusalem no longer exists, as it was destroyed by the Romans in AD 70 and never rebuilt. But faithful Jews are instructed not to go onto the Temple Mount, in case they accidentally walk into the area where the Holy of Holies was.

Further reading

James Alison, *The Joy of Being Wrong: Original sin through Easter eyes*, Hertford, NC: Crossroad Press, 1998

Paul Fiddes, *Past Event and Present Salvation*, London: DLT, 1989

Colin Gunton, *The Actuality of Atonement*, London: T&T Clark, 2003

Stephen R. Holmes, *The Wondrous Cross*, London: Paternoster, 2007

Alan Mann, *Atonement for a sinless society*, Eugene, OR: Cascade Books, 2015

John Stott, *The Cross of Christ*, Downers Grove, IL: IVP, 1986

Stephen Sykes, *The Story of Atonement*, London: DLT, 1997

T. F. Torrance, *Atonement: The person and work of Christ*, London: Paternoster, 2009 (massive tome, but hugely significant; edited posthumously by Robert T. Walker)

Frances M. Young, *Construing the Cross*, Eugene, OR: Cascade Books, 2015